Cambridge
Key English Test for Schools
1

Examination papers from
University of Cambridge
ESOL Examinations

CAMBRIDGE
UNIVERSITY PRESS

University Printing House, Cambridge CB2 8BS, United Kingdom

One Liberty Plaza, 20th Floor, New York, NY 10006, USA

477 Williamstown Road, Port Melbourne, VIC 3207, Australia

314–321, 3rd Floor, Plot 3, Splendor Forum, Jasola District Centre, New Delhi – 110025, India

79 Anson Road, #06–04/06, Singapore 079906

Cambridge University Press is part of the University of Cambridge.

It furthers the University's mission by disseminating knowledge in the pursuit of education, learning and research at the highest international levels of excellence.

www.cambridge.org
Information on this title: www.cambridge.org/9780521176828

© Cambridge University Press 2010

It is normally necessary for written permission for copying to be obtained *in advance* from a publisher. The candidate answer sheets at the back of the book are designed to be copied and distributed in class. The normal requirements are waived here and it is not necessary to write to Cambridge University Press for permission for an individual teacher to make copies for use within his or her own classroom. Only those pages which carry the wording '© UCLES 2010 Photocopiable' may be copied.

First published 2010

20 19 18 17 16

Printed in Italy by Rotolito S.p.A.

A catalogue record for this publication is available from the British Library

ISBN 978-0-521-17682-8 Student's Book without answers
ISBN 978-0-521-13992-2 Student's Book with answers
ISBN 978-0-521-14569-5 Audio CD
ISBN 978-0-521-17833-4 Self-study Pack

Cambridge University Press has no responsibility for the persistence or accuracy of URLs for external or third-party internet websites referred to in this publication, and does not guarantee that any content on such websites is, or will remain, accurate or appropriate. Information regarding prices, travel timetables and other factual information given in this work is correct at the time of first printing but Cambridge University Press does not guarantee the accuracy of such information thereafter.

Contents

Acknowledgements

A guide to KET for Schools   5

Test 1	Paper 1	14
	Paper 2	26
	Paper 3	33
Test 2	Paper 1	34
	Paper 2	46
	Paper 3	53
Test 3	Paper 1	54
	Paper 2	66
	Paper 3	73
Test 4	Paper 1	74
	Paper 2	86
	Paper 3	93

Visual materials for Paper 3   94

Sample answer sheets   102

Acknowledgements

The publishers are grateful for permission to reproduce copyright material. It has not always been possible to identify the sources of the material used, and in such cases the publishers would welcome information from the copyright owners.

Getty Images for p 18/Martin Ruegner; Photolibrary.com for pp 15/Oliver Gutfleisch, 38/Ryan Smith/Somos Images, 78/Gerhard Zwerger-Schoner; Shutterstock for pp 20/Julien Tromeur, 35/muzsy, 40/Yulia Popkova, 55/Charlie Hutton, 58/Timothy Large, 60/Maria Simonova, 75/Christopher Futcher, 80/muzsy.

Picture research by Kevin Brown

Book design by Peter Ducker MSTD

Publishing management by hyphen

The CD which accompanies this book was recorded at dsound, London.

A guide to KET for Schools

The KET for Schools examination is part of a group of general English examinations developed by Cambridge ESOL. All five examinations in this suite have similar characteristics but are designed for different levels of English language ability. Within the five levels, KET is at level A2 (Waystage) in the *Council of Europe's Common European Framework of Reference for Languages: Learning, teaching, assessment*.

Examination	Council of Europe Framework Level	UK National Qualifications Framework Level
CPE Certificate of Proficiency in English	C2	3
CAE Certificate in Advanced English	C1	2
FCE First Certificate in English	B2	1
PET for Schools Preliminary English Test	B1	Entry 3
KET for Schools Key English Test	A2	Entry 2

KET for Schools is a popular exam with candidates who are learning English out of personal interest and for those studying English as part of their school studies. It is also useful preparation for higher level exams, such as PET or PET for Schools and other Cambridge ESOL examinations. KET for Schools is an excellent first step, helping you to build your confidence in English and measure your progress. If you can deal with everyday basic written and spoken communication (for example: read simple texts, understand signs and notices, write simple notes and emails), then this is the appropriate exam for you.

There are two versions of KET available: KET and KET for Schools. KET for Schools was introduced to meet the needs of the increasing number of younger candidates taking KET. Both KET and KET for Schools follow exactly the same format and the task types, testing focuses and level of the question papers are identical. The only difference in the two versions of the exams is that the content and treatment of topics in KET for Schools are particularly targeted at the interests and experiences of younger people.

Topics

These are the topics used in the KET for Schools exam:

Clothes	Language	Shopping
Daily life	People	Social interaction
Entertainment and media	Personal feelings, opinions and experiences	Sport
Food and drink	Personal identification	The natural world
Health, medicine and exercise	Places and buildings	Transport
Hobbies and leisure	Schools and study	Travel and holidays
House and home	Services	Weather

KET for Schools content: an overview

Paper	Name	Timing	Content	Test Focus
Paper 1	Reading/Writing	1 hour 10 minutes	Nine parts: Five parts (Parts 1–5) test a range of reading skills with a variety of texts, ranging from very short notices to longer continuous texts. Parts 6–9 concentrate on testing basic writing skills.	Assessment of candidates' ability to understand the meaning of written English at word, phrase, sentence, paragraph and whole text level. Assessment of candidates' ability to produce simple written English, ranging from one-word answers to short pieces of continuous text.
Paper 2	Listening	30 minutes (including 8 minutes transfer time)	Five parts ranging from short exchanges to longer dialogues and monologues.	Assessment of candidates' ability to understand dialogues and monologues in both informal and neutral settings on a range of everyday topics.
Paper 3	Speaking	8–10 minutes per pair of candidates	Two parts: In Part 1, candidates interact with an examiner; in Part 2 they interact with another candidate.	Assessment of candidates' ability to answer and ask questions about themselves and about factual non-personal information.

Paper 1: Reading and Writing

Preparing for the Reading section

To prepare for the Reading section, you should read the type of English used in everyday life; for example, short magazine articles, advertisements, instructions, etc. It is also a good idea to practise reading short messages, including notes, emails and cards. Remember, you won't always need to understand every word to be able to do a task in the exam.

Before the exam, think about the time you need to do each part and check you know how to record your answers on the answer sheet (see page 102).

A guide to KET for Schools

Marks

Each item carries one mark, except for question 56 (Part 9), which is marked out of 5. This paper represents 50% of the total marks for the whole examination.

Reading			
Part	Task Type and Format	Task Focus	Number of questions
1	Matching. Matching 5 prompt sentences to 8 notices, plus one example.	Gist understanding of real-world notices. Reading for main message.	5
2	Three-option multiple-choice sentences. Five sentences (plus an integrated example) with connecting link of topic or story line.	Lexical. Reading and identifying appropriate vocabulary.	5
3	Three-option multiple-choice. Five discrete three-option multiple-choice items (plus an example) focusing on verbal exchange patterns. **AND** Matching. Five matching items (plus an integrated example) in a continuous dialogue, selecting from eight possible responses.	Functional language. Reading and identifying appropriate response.	10
4	Right/Wrong/Doesn't say **OR** three-option multiple-choice. One long text or three short texts adapted from authentic newspaper and magazine articles. Seven three-option multiple-choice items or seven Right/Wrong/Doesn't say items, plus an integrated example.	Reading for detailed understanding and main idea(s).	7
5	Multiple-choice cloze. A text adapted from an original source, for example, encyclopaedia entries, newspaper and magazine articles. Eight three-option multiple-choice items, plus an integrated example.	Reading and identifying appropriate structural word (auxiliary verbs, modal verbs, determiners, pronouns, prepositions, conjunctions, etc.).	8

A guide to KET for Schools

Preparing for the Writing section

To prepare for the Writing section, you should take the opportunity to write short messages in real-life situations, for example, to your teacher or to other students. These can include invitations, apologies for missing a class, notices about lost property, etc. They can be handwritten or sent as an email.

Before the exam, think about the time you need to do each part and check you know how to record your answers on the answer sheet (see page 103).

Writing			
Part	Task Type and Format	Task Focus	Number of questions
6	Word completion. Five dictionary definition type sentences (plus one integrated example). Five words to identify and spell.	Reading and identifying appropriate lexical item, and spelling.	5
7	Open cloze. Text of type candidates could be expected to write, for example, a short letter or email. Ten spaces to fill with one word (plus an integrated example) which must be spelled correctly.	Reading and identifying appropriate word with focus on structure and/or lexis.	10
8	Information transfer. Two short authentic texts (emails, adverts, etc.) to prompt completion of an output text (form, note, etc.). Five spaces to fill on output text with one or more words or numbers (plus an integrated example).	Reading and writing down appropriate words or numbers with focus on content and accuracy.	5
9	Guided writing. Either a short input text or rubric to prompt a written response. Three messages to communicate in writing.	Writing a short message, note or postcard of 25-35 words.	1

Part 6

This part is about vocabulary. You have to produce words and spell them correctly. The words will all be linked to the same topic, for example, food. You have to read a definition for each one and complete the word. The first letter is given to help you.

Part 7
This part is about grammar and vocabulary. You have to complete a short gapped text of the type you could be expected to write, for example, a note and a reply, or a short letter. You must spell all the missing words correctly.

Part 8
This part tests both reading and writing. You have to use the information in one or two short texts, for example, a note, email or advertisement, to complete a document such as a form, notice, diary entry, etc. You will need to understand the vocabulary used on forms, for example, surname, date of birth, etc. You will need to write only words or phrases in your answers, but you must spell these correctly.

Part 9
You have to write a short message (25–35 words). You are told who you are writing to and why, and you must include three content points. To gain top marks, all three points must be included in your answer, so it is important to read the question carefully and plan what you are going to write. Before the exam, practise writing answers of the correct length. You will lose marks for writing fewer than 25 words, and it is not a good idea to write answers that are too long.

Mark Scheme for Writing Part 9
There are five marks for Part 9. Minor grammatical and spelling mistakes are acceptable but to get five marks you must write a clear message and include all three content points.

Mark	Criteria	
5	All three parts of message clearly communicated. Only minor spelling errors or occasional grammatical errors.	
4	All three parts of message communicated. Some non-impeding errors in spelling and grammar or some awkwardness of expression.	
3	All three parts of message attempted. Expression requires interpretation by the reader and contains impeding errors in spelling and grammar.	Two parts of message are clearly communicated. Only minor spelling errors or occasional grammatical errors.
2	Only two parts of message communicated. Some errors in spelling and grammar. The errors in expression may require patience and interpretation by the reader and impede communication.	
1	Only one part of message communicated. Some attempt to address the task but response is very unclear.	
0	Question not attempted, or totally incomprehensible response.	

A guide to KET for Schools

Paper 2: Listening

Paper format
This paper contains 5 parts.

Number of questions
25

Task types
Matching, multiple-choice, gap-fill.

Sources
All texts are based on authentic situations, and each part is heard twice.

Answering
Candidates indicate answers either by shading lozenges (Parts 1–3) or writing answers (Parts 4 and 5) on an answer sheet.

Timing
About 30 minutes, including 8 minutes to transfer answers.

Marks
Each item carries one mark. This gives a total of 25 marks, which represents 25% of the total marks for the whole examination.

Preparing for the Listening test
The best preparation for the Listening test is to listen to authentic spoken English for your level. Apart from understanding spoken English in class, other sources include: films, TV, DVDs, songs, the internet, English clubs, and other speakers of English, such as tourists, guides, friends and family.

You will hear the instructions for each task on the recording and see them on the exam paper. There are pauses in the recording to give you time to look at the questions and to write your answers. You should write your answers on the question paper as you listen. You will have eight minutes at the end of the test to transfer your answers to the answer sheet (see page 104). Make sure you know how to do this and that you check your answers carefully.

Part	Task Type and Format	Task Focus	Number of questions
1	Three-option multiple-choice. Short neutral or informal dialogues. Five discrete three-option multiple-choice items with visuals, plus one example.	Listening to identify key information (times, prices, days of week, numbers, etc.).	5
2	Matching. Longer informal dialogue. Five items (plus one integrated example) and eight options.	Listening to identify key information.	5
3	Three-option multiple-choice. Longer informal or neutral dialogue. Five three-option multiple-choice items (plus an integrated example).	Taking the 'role' of one of the speakers and listening to identify key information.	5
4	Gap-fill. Longer neutral or informal dialogue. Five gaps to fill with one or more words or numbers, plus an integrated example. Recognisable spelling is accepted, except with very high frequency words, e.g. 'bus', 'red'; or if spelling is dictated.	Listening and writing down information (including spelling of names, places, etc., as dictated on recording).	5
5	Gap-fill. Longer neutral or informal monologue. Five gaps to fill with one or more words or numbers, plus an integrated example. Recognisable spelling is accepted, except with very high frequency words, e.g. 'bus', 'red'; or if spelling is dictated.	Listening and writing down information (including spelling of names, places, etc., as dictated on recording).	5

A guide to KET for Schools

Paper 3: Speaking

Paper format
The paper contains two parts. The standard format for Paper 3 is two candidates and two examiners. One examiner acts as an assessor and does not join in the conversation. The other is called an interlocutor and manages the interaction by asking questions and setting up the tasks.

Task types
Short exchanges with the examiner and an interactive task involving both candidates.

Timing
8–10 minutes per pair of candidates.

Marks
Candidates are assessed on their performance throughout the test. There are a total of 25 marks in Paper 3, making up 25% of the total score for the whole examination.

Preparing for the Speaking Test
Take every opportunity to practise your English with as many people as possible. Asking and answering questions in simple role plays provides useful practice. These role plays should focus on everyday language and situations and involve questions about daily activities and familiar experiences. It is also a good idea to practise exchanging information in role plays about things such as costs and opening times of, for example, a local sports centre.

Part	Task Type and Format	Length of Parts	Task Focus
1	Each candidate interacts with the interlocutor. The interlocutor asks the candidates questions. The interlocutor follows an interlocutor frame to guide the conversation, ensure standardisation and control level of input.	5–6 minutes	Language normally associated with meeting people for the first time, giving information of a factual personal kind. Bio-data type questions to respond to.
2	Candidates interact with each other. The interlocutor sets up the activity using a standardised rubric. Candidates ask and answer questions using prompt material.	3–4 minutes	Factual information of a non-personal kind, related to daily life.

A guide to KET for Schools

Assessment
You are assessed on your own individual performance and not in relation to the other candidate. Both examiners assess you – the assessor awards marks according to: Grammar and Vocabulary, Pronunciation and Interactive Communication. The interlocutor awards a mark for overall performance.

Grammar and Vocabulary
This refers to your ability to use vocabulary, structure and paraphrase strategies to convey meaning.

Pronunciation
This refers to the intelligibility of your speech. Having an accent from your first language is not penalised if it does not affect communication.

Interactive communication
This refers to your ability to take part in the interaction appropriately. Hesitation while you search for language is expected and not penalised so long as it does not strain the patience of the listener. You are given credit for being able to ask for repetition or clarification if necessary.

Global achievement
This is based on the analytical criteria and relates to your performance overall.

Further information
The information in this practice book is designed to give an overview of KET for Schools. For a full description of all of the Cambridge ESOL exams, including information about task types, testing focus and preparation, please see the relevant handbooks which can be obtained from Cambridge ESOL at the address below or from the website: www.CambridgeESOL.org

University of Cambridge ESOL Examinations
1 Hills Road
Cambridge CB1 2EU
United Kingdom
Telephone: +44 1223 553355
Fax: +44 1223 460278
Email: ESOLHelpdesk@CambridgeESOL.org

Test 1

PAPER 1 READING AND WRITING (1 hour 10 minutes)

PART 1

QUESTIONS 1–5

Which notice (**A–H**) says this (**1–5**)?
For questions **1–5**, mark the correct letter **A–H** on your answer sheet.

Example:

0   The time of this has changed.   *Answer:* | 0 | A B C D E F G H ☐☐☐☐☐■☐☐ |

---

1   You are told if your favourite team has won.

A   **Hobbs Sports Shop**
    SALE
    Starts next week

B   **Sports Centre**
    Boys' Changing Room
    (for dry sports only)

2   Come on this day and find out why sport is good for you.

C   24-hour football information line
    01894275
    All calls 5p per minute

3   You can watch a sports competition here this afternoon.

D   **Volleyball team**
    Players needed - Learn more 7 p.m. tonight
    Sports Hall

E   **Talk by school visitor**
    Play sport and stay fit
    4 p.m. March 15th

4   If you like this sport, go to the meeting this evening.

F   Earlier start for tomorrow's
    football practice
    9 a.m.

5   Some people can get ready to play tennis or football in here.

G   **EASTON SCHOOL**
    No football matches this afternoon
    Grass too wet

H   **Highgate Stadium**
    Under-14s' hockey match
    2 p.m. today

PART 2

QUESTIONS 6–10

Read the sentences about going to a concert.
Choose the best word (**A, B** or **C**) for each space.
For questions **6–10**, mark **A, B** or **C** on your answer sheet.

Example:

0   My friends and I .... to a rock concert last night.

    A   followed   **B**   went   **C**   arrived   *Answer:* **0** A ■ C

---

6   The concert began at seven and we didn't want to be ....

    A   late   **B**   soon   **C**   already

7   At the concert, we .... the words to most of the songs.

    A   believed   **B**   knew   **C**   thought

8   The music was very .... so we couldn't chat to one another.

    A   full   **B**   hard   **C**   loud

9   The band .... on stage for over two hours.

    A   stayed   **B**   passed   **C**   spent

10   We all .... a great time at the concert.

    A   did   **B**   had   **C**   put

PART 3

QUESTIONS 11–15

Complete the five conversations.
For questions **11–15**, mark **A**, **B** or **C** on your answer sheet.

Example:

0

Where do you come from?

- **A** New York.
- **B** School.
- **C** Home.

Answer: 0 ■ A □ B □ C

---

11 What about going to the cinema this evening?

- **A** I really enjoyed it.
- **B** I'm certain.
- **C** I'd love to.

12 We had a wonderful time on holiday.

- **A** Where did you go?
- **B** Why did you do that?
- **C** Have you been there?

13 If I buy a book for Mum, will you buy her some flowers?

- **A** But I've already got her something else.
- **B** If you do too.
- **C** Did you get them in town yesterday?

14 I'm sorry I forgot your birthday.

- **A** It's mine.
- **B** It doesn't matter.
- **C** It won't be.

15 What's your new teacher like?

- **A** Maths and tennis.
- **B** Three lessons a week.
- **C** Very nice, I think.

QUESTIONS 16–20

Complete the conversation.

What does Sara say to her mother?

For questions **16–20**, mark the correct letter **A–H** on your answer sheet.

Example:

Mother: Sara, please stop watching TV.

Sara: 0 .....D......

Answer: 0 [D marked]

Mother: Sorry, but I need you to come and help me now.

Sara: **16** ....

Mother: Help me with some cooking. I've got lots to do before Saturday.

Sara: **17** ....

Mother: Your uncle and his family are going to visit us.

Sara: **18** ....

Mother: Well, they are and I need to get things ready.

Sara: **19** ....

Mother: Good idea. Have we got any eggs?

Sara: **20** ....

Mother: Great. You can get started then.

A Shall I make a cake then?

B They've already done that.

C Why? Is something special happening at the weekend?

D Just a bit longer, Mum.

E I made them a chocolate one.

F Do you? What would you like me to do?

G I think so. Yes, here they are.

H I didn't know they were coming.

PART 4

QUESTIONS 21–27

Read the article about a young swimmer.

Are sentences **21–27** 'Right' **(A)** or 'Wrong' **(B)**?

If there is not enough information to answer 'Right' **(A)** or 'Wrong' **(B)**, choose 'Doesn't say' **(C)**.

For questions **21–27**, mark **A**, **B** or **C** on your answer sheet.

Canada's top young swimmer

Greg Rye, the young Canadian swimmer, is becoming more and more famous. He has his own teacher, driver and even his own cook. Each time people hear him speak on television, they can't believe he's only 13. Greg's father is an engineer but he is also his son's manager. He says, 'I don't make Greg do anything he doesn't want to do. He chooses which competitions to swim in. But he works hard to keep fit and wins nearly every race he's in. I cut out all the newspaper articles about him and put them in a big box!'

Greg's phone rings several times a day because people want to write about him or photograph him for magazines. 'When I'm at school,' Greg says, 'I just want to be like my classmates. That's really important to me.' But Greg doesn't have a normal schoolboy's life. He often has to travel for international races and has little free time. 'I go to the pool every day and swim there for at least six hours. I get angry sometimes if I can't go to a party or spend time with friends because I have to swim or rest, but when I'm in the pool, I love every minute.'

Paper 1 Reading and Writing

Example:

0   A lot of people know who Greg Rye is.

   A   Right   B   Wrong   C   Doesn't say   Answer: 0 A ■ B □ C □

---

21   Greg has only been on TV once.

   A   Right   B   Wrong   C   Doesn't say

22   People think that Greg is older than he really is.

   A   Right   B   Wrong   C   Doesn't say

23   Greg's father works as an engineer three days a week.

   A   Right   B   Wrong   C   Doesn't say

24   Greg's father tells him which races to swim in.

   A   Right   B   Wrong   C   Doesn't say

25   Greg's father keeps the articles that journalists have written about his son.

   A   Right   B   Wrong   C   Doesn't say

26   Greg is popular with his classmates.

   A   Right   B   Wrong   C   Doesn't say

27   Greg always has time to go to parties with his friends.

   A   Right   B   Wrong   C   Doesn't say

PART 5

QUESTIONS 28–35

Read the article about robots.

Choose the best word (**A**, **B** or **C**) for each space.

For questions **28–35**, mark **A**, **B** or **C** on your answer sheet.

Robots

Most people have seen films **(0)** .... robots, but robots are also used in real life. Robots can do **(28)** .... different things. They can, for example, make things in factories **(29)** .... help astronauts in space.

One new robot from Japan can **(30)** .... walk, run and climb stairs. Engineers hope that in the future **(31)** .... robot will be able to help people in their homes. **(32)** .... new robot is special because it can have a conversation **(33)** .... you.

A Canadian scientist has just **(34)** .... a robot that has hands that can move in 24 different ways. This is easy for people but **(35)** .... now it wasn't possible for a robot to do this.

Example:

| 0 | **A** | about | **B** | in | **C** | over | *Answer:* | 0 A■ B☐ C☐ |

28	**A**	lots	**B**	much	**C**	many
29	**A**	or	**B**	because	**C**	if
30	**A**	ever	**B**	even	**C**	yet
31	**A**	some	**B**	this	**C**	these
32	**A**	Other	**B**	Both	**C**	Another
33	**A**	for	**B**	to	**C**	with
34	**A**	made	**B**	making	**C**	makes
35	**A**	since	**B**	until	**C**	from

PART 6

QUESTIONS 36–40

Read the descriptions of some words about health and the body.
What is the word for each one?
The first letter is already there. There is one space for each other letter in the word.
For questions **36–40**, write the words on your answer sheet.

Example:

0   This person can help you if you don't feel well.   d _ _ _ _ _

Answer: | 0 | *doctor* |

36   You have to look in the mirror to see this part of your body.   f _ _ _

37   If you have long hair, you need to use this every day.   b _ _ _ _

38   If you eat this fruit once a day you will stay healthy.   a _ _ _ _

39   People use this to wash themselves.   s _ _ _

40   People are taken to hospital in this when they are ill.   a _ _ _ _ _ _ _

PART 7

QUESTIONS 41–50

Complete the email.
Write ONE word for each space.
For questions **41–50**, write the words on your answer sheet.

Example: | **0** | b e |

| **From:** | Ivan |
| **To:** | Roberto |

Hi Roberto,

It'll **(0)** .... my 12th birthday on June 18th. We are **(41)** .... to have a barbecue at the lake. We'll have **(42)** .... fun there than at the park. Would you **(43)** .... to come? My dad will take us there **(44)** .... car and he says I can invite some **(45)** .... my friends.

Janet has already said she can come and I'm also inviting Ian **(46)** .... you. You don't **(47)** .... to bring anything to **(48)** .... or drink because my mum will make a picnic.

(49) .... it's warm and sunny we will go for a swim in the lake, so don't forget **(50)** .... bring your swimming things.

PART 8

QUESTIONS 51–55

Read the website advertisement and the email.

Fill in the information in Mark's notes.

For questions **51–55**, write the information on your answer sheet.

Top Two Books
this month:

Forest Street
by Alan Banks
and
Best Bike Rides
by Kim James

Order before 10th April for
special price for both books – £20
www.booksalot.com

From: Tony
To: Mark

Let's get Laurie a book for his birthday. The new cycling book which is on sale at www.booksalot.com looks good, but it must arrive before April 12th, so can you order it online tonight?

It's £12.90 so that will cost us £6.45 each. Is that OK? I'll give you the money next week. Get them to post it to 39 West Road.

Thanks.

MARK'S NOTES

Laurie's birthday present

Website:	www.booksalot.com
Name of book:	**51**
Writer:	**52**
Date needed by:	**53**
Address to send book to:	**54**
Price of book:	**55** £

PART 9

QUESTION 56

You went to a friend's house yesterday and you left your bag there.
Write an email to your English friend, Jay.

Say:
- **what colour** the bag is
- **what** is **inside** the bag
- **where** in the house **you left it**.

Write **25–35** words.
Write the email on your answer sheet.

PAPER 2 LISTENING (approximately 30 minutes including 8 minutes transfer time)

PART 1

QUESTIONS 1–5

You will hear five short conversations.

You will hear each conversation twice.

There is one question for each conversation.

For each question, choose the right answer (**A**, **B** or **C**).

Example:

Which is the girl's horse?

A

B

C

---

1 What's Sally doing now?

A

B

C

2 Where did the woman find the ball?

A

B

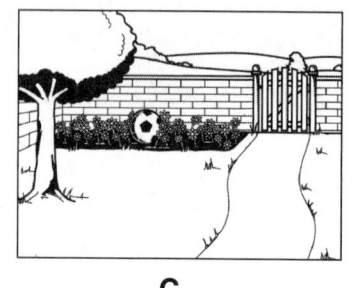

C

Paper 2   Listening

3 How will Bella get to her friend's house this afternoon?

A

B

C

4 What job does Mark's sister do?

A

B

C

5 What's the date of Adrian's birthday party?

A

B

C

Test 1

PART 2

QUESTIONS 6–10

Listen to Sam talking to a friend about his family.
Which sport does each person do now?
For questions **6–10**, write a letter **A–H** next to each person.
You will hear the conversation twice.

Example:

| 0 | grandfather | F |

PEOPLE

6   father   ☐

7   brother   ☐

8   uncle   ☐

9   sister   ☐

10 mother   ☐

SPORTS THEY DO NOW

A   climbing

B   football

C   hockey

D   sailing

E   skiing

F   swimming

G   tennis

H   volleyball

PART 3

QUESTIONS 11–15

Listen to Emma talking to a friend about her photography course.
For each question, choose the right answer (**A**, **B** or **C**).
You will hear the conversation twice.

Example:

0   Where does Emma do her photography course?

      A   Parkplace School

      (**B**)   Riverside School

      C   West School

---

11   The photography classes start at

      A   2.00 p.m.

      B   2.30 p.m.

      C   2.45 p.m.

12   Emma's photography course costs

      A   £45.

      B   £65.

      C   £80.

13   Emma likes the course because she's

      A   learning about famous photographers.

      B   using an expensive camera.

      C   taking better photographs.

14 Emma thinks it's easy to take photographs of

    A flowers.

    B animals.

    C people.

15 What does Emma want to do after the course?

    A buy a digital camera

    B take photos for a competition

    C show her photos to her friends

PART 4

QUESTIONS 16–20

You will hear a boy, Richard, talking to a friend about visiting the circus.

Listen and complete each question.

You will hear the conversation twice.

Going to the Circus

Name of circus: Zippo's

Day of circus visit: (16) ....

Time show finishes: (17) .... p.m.

Travel there by: (18) ....

Cost of a ticket: (19) £ ....

Take: (20) ....

Test 1

PART 5
QUESTIONS 21–25

You will hear a teacher giving some information about a trip to a museum.
Listen and complete each question.
You will hear the information twice.

Museum Trip

Name of museum:	The Fashion Museum
Time bus leaves:	**(21)** .... a.m.
At 2 p.m. see:	**(22)** fashion ....
Must take:	**(23)** ....
Cost of my ticket:	**(24)** £ ....
Date of trip:	**(25)** ....

You now have 8 minutes to write your answers on the answer sheet.

PAPER 3 SPEAKING (8–10 minutes)

The Speaking test lasts 8 to 10 minutes. You will take the test with another candidate. There are two examiners, but only one of them will talk to you. The examiner will ask you questions and ask you to talk to the other candidate.

Part 1 (5–6 minutes)

The examiner will ask you and your partner some questions. These questions will be about your daily life, past experience and future plans. For example, you may have to speak about your school, hobbies or home town.

Part 2 (3–4 minutes)

You and your partner will speak to each other. You will ask and answer questions. The examiner will give you a card with some information on it. The examiner will give your partner a card with some words on it. Your partner will use the words on the card to ask you questions about the information you have. Then you will change roles.

Test 2

PAPER 1 READING AND WRITING (1 hour 10 minutes)

PART 1

QUESTIONS 1–5

Which notice (**A–H**) says this (**1–5**)?
For questions **1–5**, mark the correct letter **A–H** on your answer sheet.

Example:

0 There is nobody at work here in the middle of the day.

Answer: **0** A B C D E F **G** H

---

1 Young people and their parents may choose different meals.

A There is no restaurant on today's 12.30 train

B This way to the restaurant garden

2 People who are travelling can get something to eat here.

C Alco Department Store
Half-price cups and glasses
Today only

3 If you need some of these for your kitchen, you should buy them now.

D Station Café
Open all day
Opposite ticket office

E **CITY SCHOOL**
Indian and Chinese cooking lessons begin Monday

4 You may get a present when you eat here.

F *Riverside Restaurant*
Ask the waiter for our special children's menu

5 You can learn how to make different kinds of food here.

G School office closed for lunch between 1 p.m. and 2 p.m.

H Marco's Pizzeria
Free toy with every under-12's meal

PART 2

QUESTIONS 6–10

Read the sentences about a girl who likes volleyball.
Choose the best word (**A**, **B** or **C**) for each space.
For questions **6–10**, mark **A**, **B** or **C** on your answer sheet.

Example:

0   Diana .... a lot of time playing volleyball for her school.

   A   spends   B   uses   C   gives

   Answer: 0 **A** ☐ ☐

---

6   Diana's team .... volleyball three times a week.

   A   exercises   B   practises   C   tries

7   At a match last week, Diana won a silver .... for being the best player.

   A   cup   B   glass   C   can

8   Diana sometimes has to .... school when her team travels to play against other teams.

   A   fail   B   lose   C   miss

9   Diana is .... that her team will do well this year.

   A   certain   B   careful   C   correct

10 Diana would like to .... a famous sportswoman one day.

   A   start   B   get   C   become

PART 3

QUESTIONS 11–15

Complete the five conversations.
For questions **11–15**, mark **A**, **B** or **C** on your answer sheet.

Example:

0

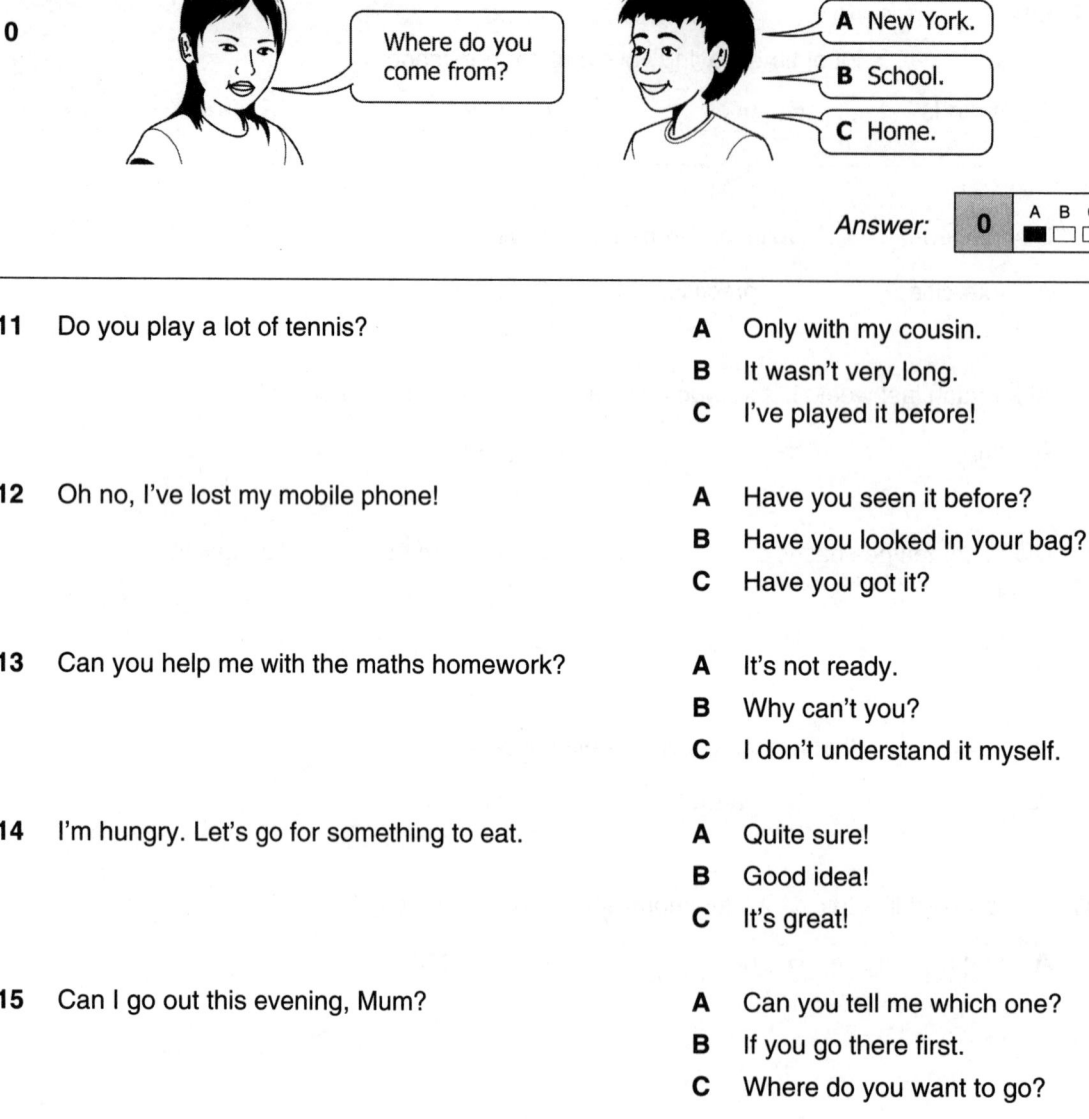

Where do you come from?

A New York.
B School.
C Home.

Answer: 0 A ■ B □ C □

---

11 Do you play a lot of tennis?

A Only with my cousin.
B It wasn't very long.
C I've played it before!

12 Oh no, I've lost my mobile phone!

A Have you seen it before?
B Have you looked in your bag?
C Have you got it?

13 Can you help me with the maths homework?

A It's not ready.
B Why can't you?
C I don't understand it myself.

14 I'm hungry. Let's go for something to eat.

A Quite sure!
B Good idea!
C It's great!

15 Can I go out this evening, Mum?

A Can you tell me which one?
B If you go there first.
C Where do you want to go?

QUESTIONS 16–20

Complete the telephone conversation between two friends.
What does Mark say to Josh?
For questions **16–20**, mark the correct letter **A–H** on your answer sheet.

Example:

Josh: Hi Mark. What are you doing this evening?

Mark: 0 ....E....

Answer: 0 [E marked]

Josh: Do you want to go to the cinema later?

Mark: 16 ....

Josh: I'm not sure but we can go to the cinema and choose the best one.

Mark: 17 ....

Josh: OK. I'll see you as soon as I finish the maths homework.

Mark: 18 ....

Josh: OK, shall I come to your house at 7 p.m. then?

Mark: 19 ....

Josh: No problem, I'll do my homework quickly. How much money will I need?

Mark: 20 ....

Josh: Oh, great! See you later.

A That won't take you long. I've already done it and it's easy.

B It's OK, my mum's given me some money.

C Do you like that cinema?

D All right. Why don't you come to my house first and we'll walk there together.

E Not much. Why?

F Maybe. Do you know which films are showing?

G It's a great film.

H Can you get here a bit earlier than that?

PART 4

QUESTIONS 21–27

Read the article about some girls who play in a band.

Are sentences **21–27** 'Right' **(A)** or 'Wrong' **(B)**?

If there is not enough information to answer 'Right' **(A)** or 'Wrong' **(B)**, choose 'Doesn't say' **(C)**.

For questions **21–27**, mark **A**, **B** or **C** on your answer sheet.

Our Band

Fourteen-year-old Emma Peters talks about her new band

Soon it will be the summer holidays again. I'm not going away with my parents this year but I don't mind. I'm going to spend most of my time with two of my classmates, Bella and Lou.

We've just started a rock band which we call Sunshine. I play the guitar and sing, Bella plays the guitar and the keyboard and Lou plays the drums. We practise in Lou's dad's garage and we also play in music shops and local cafés. The band has been together for four months and we're all very good friends. I was in a different band last year but that wasn't so much fun. No one wanted to practise.

We've written several songs and we have our own website. Over the summer we are going to make a CD with ten or maybe twelve songs on it. We're not sure yet. We haven't finished writing all the songs, but we've decided on the name of the CD. We're going to call it *The Red Room*. The CD may not make us famous, but that doesn't matter – we just enjoy our music and sharing it with other people. I can't think of a better way to spend the summer.

Paper 1 Reading and Writing

Example:

0   Emma's summer holiday has already begun.

   A   Right   **B**   Wrong   **C**   Doesn't say   *Answer:* [0] A ☐ B ■ C ☐

---

21   Emma would like to go somewhere with her family this summer.

   A   Right   **B**   Wrong   **C**   Doesn't say

22   Emma goes to the same school as the other members of the band, Sunshine.

   A   Right   **B**   Wrong   **C**   Doesn't say

23   Each of the three girls in the band plays an instrument.

   A   Right   **B**   Wrong   **C**   Doesn't say

24   The band is paid for playing in shops and cafés.

   A   Right   **B**   Wrong   **C**   Doesn't say

25   Emma says that her first band worked very hard.

   A   Right   **B**   Wrong   **C**   Doesn't say

26   The three girls have decided how many songs their CD will have.

   A   Right   **B**   Wrong   **C**   Doesn't say

27   The three girls hope their CD will make them famous.

   A   Right   **B**   Wrong   **C**   Doesn't say

Test 2

PART 5

QUESTIONS 28–35

Read the article about learning to snowboard.
Choose the best word (**A**, **B** or **C**) for each space.
For questions **28–35**, mark **A**, **B** or **C** on your answer sheet.

Learning to snowboard

If you want to learn to snowboard, **(0)** .... first thing you need to do is book **(28)** .... lessons. It's a good idea to have lessons with a snowboard school **(29)** .... you need to learn the right way to snowboard. You will have much **(30)** .... fun learning with other people as well.

Indoor snow schools usually **(31)** .... you a snowboard, boots and a helmet to wear on your head **(32)** .... lessons. The indoor centres are cold and use real snow, so warm clothes are important. It's not a good idea to wear jeans because **(33)** .... get wet easily.

If you learn outside on a mountain, you **(34)** .... to take your own board and boots or rent them. You will **(35)** .... need sunglasses, gloves and a helmet.

40

Example:

| 0 | **A** a | **B** one | **C** the | *Answer:* | 0 ■ |

| 28 | **A** each | **B** some | **C** any |

| 29 | **A** or | **B** and | **C** because |

| 30 | **A** more | **B** many | **C** most |

| 31 | **A** given | **B** give | **C** giving |

| 32 | **A** during | **B** among | **C** into |

| 33 | **A** them | **B** their | **C** they |

| 34 | **A** must | **B** have | **C** can |

| 35 | **A** too | **B** quite | **C** also |

Test 2

PART 6

QUESTIONS 36–40

Read the descriptions of some things you find in a living room.
What is the word for each one?
The first letter is already there. There is one space for each other letter in the word.
For questions **36–40**, write the words on your answer sheet.

Example:

0 You can watch programmes on this.   t _ _ _ _ _ _ _ _ _

Answer: | **0** | t e l e v i s i o n |

---

36 This is a comfortable seat for two or more people.   s _ _ _ _

37 If you want to know the time, you need to look at this.   c _ _ _ _ _

38 This usually has green leaves and you can grow it inside a house.   p _ _ _ _

39 People turn this on when it is dark.   l _ _ _ _

40 If you have a drink or snack, you can put it down on this.   t _ _ _ _

PART 7

QUESTIONS 41–50

Complete the email.

Write ONE word for each space.

For questions **41–50**, write the words on your answer sheet.

Example: | **0** | *for* |

From:	Lara
To:	Rebecca

Hi Rebecca,

Thank you **(0)** ………… your email. **(41)** ………… you busy on Saturday? **(42)** ………… you like to come shopping with me? My cousin is **(43)** ………… to have a party at her place **(44)** ………… week and I don't have anything nice to wear.

I want to buy a new pair **(45)** ………… jeans and maybe a T-shirt as well. **(46)** ………… you know a good shop? It has **(47)** ………… be quite a cheap place because I've only got £25.

(48) ………… you can come, I'll meet you at your house. Is the morning **(49)** ………… afternoon better for you?

Text and let **(50)** ………… know.

Lara

Test 2

PART 8

QUESTIONS 51–55

Read the advertisement and the email.

Fill in the information in José's notes.

For questions **51–55**, write the information on your answer sheet.

EXHIBITIONS AT CITY MUSEUM

10–14 June
Pyramid Treasures

18–21 June
Aztec Gold

Tickets:
Adult: £ 6.50
Students: £ 4.00

From: Carlos
To: José

The Pyramid Treasures exhibition has just finished so let's go to the Aztec Gold one – we can go on the exhibition's first day. It starts at 10 a.m. so I'll see you at the park nearby at 9.30 a.m. and we'll walk to the museum together. We can get the cheaper tickets because we're still at school.

JOSÉ'S NOTES

Exhibition visit

Place:	City Museum
Name of exhibition:	**51**
Date of visit:	**52**
My ticket price:	**53** £
Time to meet Carlos:	**54** a.m.
Place to meet Carlos:	**55**

PART 9

QUESTION 56

Yesterday you went to the sports stadium in your town.
Write an email to your English friend, Alex.

Say:
- **who went with you** to the stadium
- **which sport** you watched there
- **how long** you stayed there.

Write **25–35** words.
Write the email on your answer sheet.

PAPER 2   LISTENING   (approximately 30 minutes including 8 minutes transfer time)

PART 1
QUESTIONS 1–5

You will hear five short conversations.

You will hear each conversation twice.

There is one question for each conversation.

For each question, choose the right answer (**A**, **B** or **C**).

Example:

Which is the girl's horse?

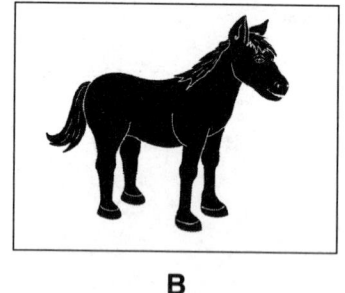

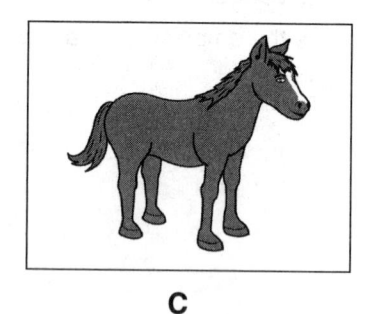

A B C

1   Where is William's mobile?

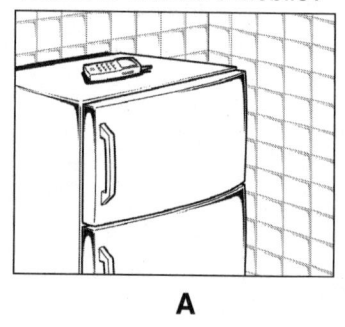

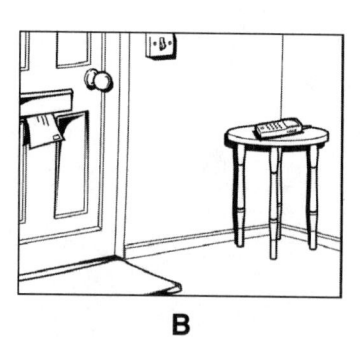

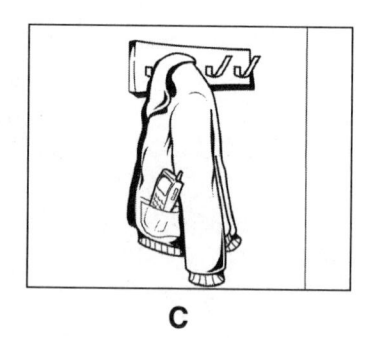

A B C

2   How much is a ticket for today's match?

£2.50   £4.00   £5.00

A B C

3 Which is the boy's sister?

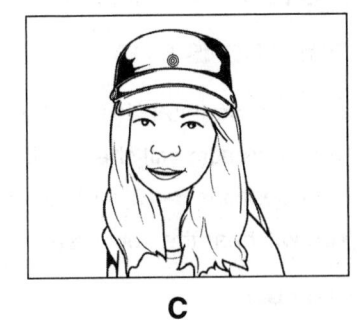

A   B   C

4 Where will they meet?

A   B   C

5 What will they do this evening?

A   B   C

PART 2

QUESTIONS 6–10

Listen to Sophie talking to her mother about presents for the family.
Which present will she buy for each person?
For questions **6–10**, write a letter **A–H** next to each person.
You will hear the conversation twice.

Example:

0   Nick   E

PEOPLE

6   Dad

7   Uncle Tim

8   Grandpa

9   Max

10 Ben

PRESENTS

A   hat

B   jacket

C   pen

D   shirt

E   socks

F   sweater

G   T-shirt

H   watch

PART 3

QUESTIONS 11–15

Listen to Jay talking to a friend about a holiday he went on with his family.

For each question, choose the right answer (**A**, **B** or **C**).

You will hear the conversation twice.

Example:

0   Jay came back from holiday on

      A   Friday.

      B   Saturday.

     (**C**)   Sunday.

---

11   The hotel Jay stayed in was

      A   in a city centre.

      B   near the sea.

      C   in the mountains.

12   Jay often spent his time

      A   playing tennis.

      B   swimming.

      C   playing golf.

13   Jay's room had

      A   a computer.

      B   a fridge.

      C   a television.

14 Jay ate a lot of

    A pasta.

    B fish.

    C salads.

15 Jay's parents thought the hotel was

    A too expensive.

    B very comfortable.

    C too noisy.

PART 4

QUESTIONS 16–20

You will hear Maria talking to her teacher about a school hockey competition.

Listen and complete each question.

You will hear the conversation twice.

Hockey Competition

Day of competition:	Tuesday
Arrive at school at:	(16) .... a.m.
High School teacher's name:	(17) Mr ....
Take players to:	(18) school ....
Bring:	(19) £ .... for a snack
Number of schools in competition:	(20) ....

PART 5

QUESTIONS 21–25

You will hear a man leaving a message about a bike.
Listen and complete each question.
You will hear the information twice.

Message

Name of person calling:	John
Day to collect bike:	(21) ....
Colour of bike:	(22) ....
Price of bike:	(23) £ ....
Address to go to:	(24) .... North Street
Time shop closes:	(25) .... p.m.

You now have 8 minutes to write your answers on the answer sheet.

PAPER 3 SPEAKING (8–10 minutes)

The Speaking test lasts 8 to 10 minutes. You will take the test with another candidate. There are two examiners, but only one of them will talk to you. The examiner will ask you questions and ask you to talk to the other candidate.

Part 1 (5–6 minutes)

The examiner will ask you and your partner some questions. These questions will be about your daily life, past experience and future plans. For example, you may have to speak about your school, hobbies or home town.

Part 2 (3–4 minutes)

You and your partner will speak to each other. You will ask and answer questions. The examiner will give you a card with some information on it. The examiner will give your partner a card with some words on it. Your partner will use the words on the card to ask you questions about the information you have. Then you will change roles.

Test 3

PAPER 1 READING AND WRITING (1 hour 10 minutes)

PART 1

QUESTIONS 1–5

Which notice **(A–H)** says this **(1–5)**?
For questions **1–5**, mark the correct letter **A–H** on your answer sheet.

Example:

0 You don't have to pay for your drink.   *Answer:* [0] A **B** C D E F G H

---

1 You can learn to cook here.

A Volleyball team needs 3 more players
Call John Linton (660581)

2 It will not be possible to buy food here this morning.

B **Today only**
Free can of lemonade
with all burger meals

3 Talk to this person if you are interested in this sport.

C **DANGER**
No cooking on fires or
barbecues on this beach

D SCHOOL SNACK SHOP ONLY OPEN
12 – 3 P.M. TODAY

4 You can buy healthy drinks in this place.

E **Green's Sports Club**
New exercise class
Join now – all ages welcome

5 If you want to get fit, go here to become a member.

F **Hockey Team Meeting**
Saturday, 10 a.m.
All players must come!

G **Fruit Juice Bar**
Special today –
banana and white grape

H **Newtown School**
Course starts Saturday
Making Italian food

PART 2

QUESTIONS 6–10

Read the sentences about a boy who likes cars.
Choose the best word (**A**, **B** or **C**) for each space.
For questions **6–10**, mark **A**, **B** or **C** on your answer sheet.

Example:

0   Victor's .... lesson at school is science.

    A   favourite   **B**   popular   **C**   excellent   *Answer:* 0 [A■ B☐ C☐]

---

6   Last week, Victor's science teacher .... to the class how cars work.

    A   spoke   **B**   explained   **C**   said

7   Victor's class now know about different .... of car engines.

    A   ways   **B**   things   **C**   kinds

8   Victor has .... posters of cars all over his bedroom walls.

    A   put   **B**   made   **C**   taken

9   Victor .... last Saturday morning cleaning his dad's new sports car.

    A   kept   **B**   spent   **C**   left

10   When Victor is older he .... to be a racing driver or an engineer.

    A   believes   **B**   thinks   **C**   hopes

PART 3

QUESTIONS 11–15

Complete the five conversations.
For questions 11–15, mark **A**, **B** or **C** on your answer sheet.

Example:

0 Where do you come from?
 - A New York.
 - B School.
 - C Home.

Answer: 0 — A

---

11 Are you feeling better today?
 - A Much, thanks.
 - B Most of it.
 - C More than me.

12 I've lost my school bag.
 - A Are you sure?
 - B I don't think it is.
 - C How do you do?

13 What shall we do when we get to the park?
 - A We have to walk to it.
 - B We will do some of them.
 - C We can play tennis.

14 I didn't see you on the bus this morning.
 - A It was very quick.
 - B I walked here today.
 - C I didn't see it.

15 Why don't you send her an email?
 - A I'd like to read it.
 - B I'll do it now.
 - C It's better than that one.

QUESTIONS 16–20

Complete the conversation between two friends.
What does Chris say to Nick?
For questions **16–20**, mark the correct letter **A–H** on your answer sheet.

Example:

Nick: Hello, Chris. How are you?
Chris: 0 .....F.....

Answer: 0 — F

Nick: Not bad, but I've got a lot of maths homework to do tonight.

Chris: 16 ....

Nick: My laptop's broken. I'm going to Jack's house to use his.

Chris: 17 ....

Nick: It's quite a long bus journey from here.

Chris: 18 ....

Nick: Are you sure? Don't you need it this evening?

Chris: 19 ....

Nick: Really? That sounds great. And you're good at maths.

Chris: 20 ....

Nick: You'll be able to help me, of course!

A   I suppose I am, but why do you say that?

B   How far away is that?

C   It's easier than everything else.

D   What's wrong with your computer?

E   So why aren't you at home doing it now?

F   OK thanks, Nick. And you?

G   It's fine, I can use my brother's instead.

H   Well, my house is nearer. Why don't you come and use my computer?

PART 4

QUESTIONS 21–27

Read the article about a young girl who enjoys riding a BMX bike.

Are sentences **21–27** 'Right' **(A)** or 'Wrong' **(B)**?

If there is not enough information to answer 'Right' **(A)** or 'Wrong' **(B)**, choose 'Doesn't say' **(C)**.

For questions **21–27**, mark **A**, **B** or **C** on your answer sheet.

BMX Racing

Lisa Hawkins loves riding her BMX bike and her dream is to go to the Olympics.

Lisa first got interested in BMX racing when she went to watch her cousins in a competition at the age of ten. She hired a bike there for a pound and immediately fell in love with the sport. 'It was the best pound I ever spent,' she says. Lisa is only 16 but she has already had lots of success, and got first prize in a world BMX competition last year.

BMX racing is quite a dangerous sport and last year Lisa broke her shoulder and her foot. This did not stop her wanting to do more competitions. She exercises every day. She rides her bike for three hours or more and sometimes she goes to the gym or the swimming pool as well.

Like many sports people, Lisa believes in luck as well as hard work. 'My mother gave me a toy rabbit and I took it to the first competition that I won. Now I take it with me everywhere I go. I'm sure that it brings me luck because the one day I left it at home, I broke my foot!'

Example:

0   Lisa Hawkins raced at the last Olympics.

    A   Right   **B**   Wrong   **C**   Doesn't say

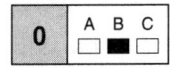

21   Lisa is the only person in her family who rides a BMX.

    A   Right   **B**   Wrong   **C**   Doesn't say

22   Lisa liked the sport the first time she tried it.

    A   Right   **B**   Wrong   **C**   Doesn't say

23   Lisa has already won an international BMX competition.

    A   Right   **B**   Wrong   **C**   Doesn't say

24   Lisa was riding her favourite bike when she had an accident.

    A   Right   **B**   Wrong   **C**   Doesn't say

25   Lisa cycles less than three hours every day.

    A   Right   **B**   Wrong   **C**   Doesn't say

26   Lisa's mother always goes to competitions with her.

    A   Right   **B**   Wrong   **C**   Doesn't say

27   Lisa once forgot to take her lucky rabbit with her.

    A   Right   **B**   Wrong   **C**   Doesn't say

PART 5

QUESTIONS 28–35

Read the article about sleep.
Choose the best word (**A**, **B** or **C**) for each space.
For questions **28–35**, mark **A**, **B** or **C** on your answer sheet.

Teenagers and sleep

Teenagers need **(0)** .... lot of sleep. As a teenager you should sleep one hour more each day **(28)** .... you did when you were younger. Your body grows quickly during these years and this means that you need **(29)** .... nine and eleven hours of sleep.

To get **(30)** .... sleep, you should usually go to bed before 10.30 p.m. **(31)** .... night. It doesn't matter **(32)** .... it is a school night or a weekend night. Your body still needs **(33)** .... sleep.

Most teenagers only get around six hours' sleep, **(34)** .... explains why they find it so difficult to get up early in the morning. When you don't get the sleep you need, you **(35)** .... feel unhappy and find it difficult to learn.

Example:

| 0 | A | the | B | a | C | one | Answer: | 0 [A☐ B■ C☐] |

28	A	than	B	like	C	as
29	A	from	B	until	C	between
30	A	enough	B	many	C	another
31	A	some	B	every	C	all
32	A	so	B	because	C	if
33	A	its	B	his	C	their
34	A	that	B	which	C	who
35	A	must	B	should	C	may

PART 6

QUESTIONS 36–40

Read the descriptions of some places in a city.
What is the word for each one?
The first letter is already there. There is one space for each other letter in the word.
For questions **36–40**, write the words on your answer sheet.

Example:

| 0 | Students are taught in classrooms here. | c _ _ _ _ _ _ |

Answer: | 0 | college |

| 36 | If you have a special card, you can take books home from here. | l _ _ _ _ _ _ |

| 37 | You can order a meal in this place. | r _ _ _ _ _ _ _ _ |

| 38 | This is a large building and things like cars are made here. | f _ _ _ _ _ _ |

| 39 | You can look at interesting old things in this building. | m _ _ _ _ _ |

| 40 | This store sells everything you need for cooking and cleaning. | s _ _ _ _ _ _ _ _ _ |

PART 7

QUESTIONS 41–50

Complete the message left on the internet.
Write ONE word for each space.
For questions **41–50**, write the words on your answer sheet.

Example: | **0** | is |

My name **(0)** ………… Teresa Lopez. I live in the centre of Buenos Aires and I'm twelve **(41)** ………… a half years old.

I enjoy school. I'm good **(42)** ………… music and languages but I hate history. The lessons **(43)** ………… so boring. When I'm older, I want to **(44)** ………… a film star or a dancer but my parents **(45)** ………… not think that's a good idea!

I like meeting lots **(46)** ………… different people, and I'd like to travel all around the world. I **(47)** ………… only been to the USA, but next summer I hope **(48)** ………… visit Europe. That's why I'm looking **(49)** ………… a penfriend in England.

Please send me an email and tell me **(50)** ………… your family and your hobbies.

PART 8

QUESTIONS 51–55

Read the notice and the email.
Fill in the information on the class trip booking form.
For questions **51–55**, write the information on your answer sheet.

CLASS TRIP

February 28 – Fashion Show
OR
March 3 – Leeds Castle

Each trip costs £14
No more than £5 spending money please

Bus leaves from school at 7.30 a.m.

**Phone School Secretary (441553)
for more information.**

From:	Becky Elliott
To:	Emma Watson

I can't come to school tomorrow. Can you fill in my class trip form? I think the fashion show sounds better than the castle trip and please give them mum's work number (287229). I usually prefer travelling by train but this bus journey will be OK because it won't take long.

CLASS TRIP BOOKING FORM

Student's name: Becky Elliott

Trip to: **51**

Travel by: **52**

Date: **53**

Price: **54** £

Parent's phone number: **55**

PART 9

QUESTION 56

Read the email from your English friend, Alex.

From:	Alex
To:	

I'd love to come to your party. What time does it start? Where is it? What shall I bring?

Write an email to Alex and answer the questions.

Write **25–35** words.

Write the email on your answer sheet.

PAPER 2 LISTENING (approximately 30 minutes including 8 minutes transfer time)

PART 1

QUESTIONS 1–5

You will hear five short conversations.

You will hear each conversation twice.

There is one question for each conversation.

For each question, choose the right answer (**A**, **B** or **C**).

Example:

Which is the girl's horse?

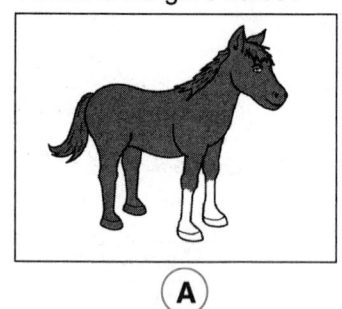

A B C

---

1 What doesn't the girl like about her photo?

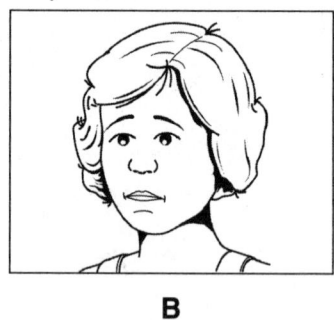

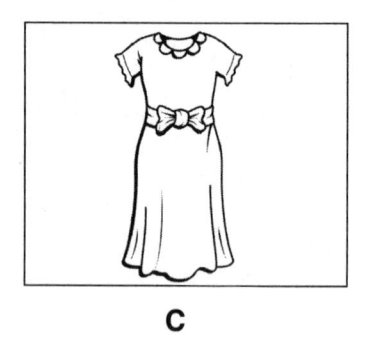

A B C

2 What will Tim do first?

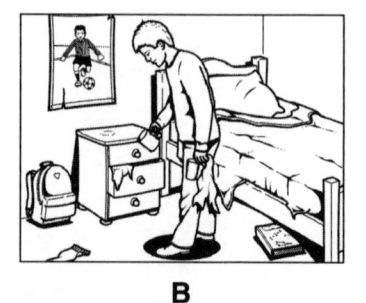

A B C

3 Which is the girl's next lesson?

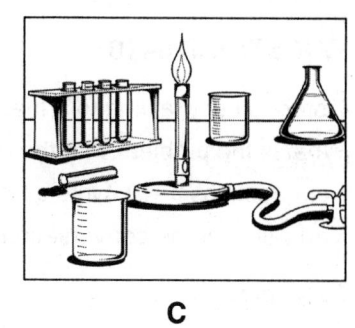

A   B   C

4 What is Sonia going to eat?

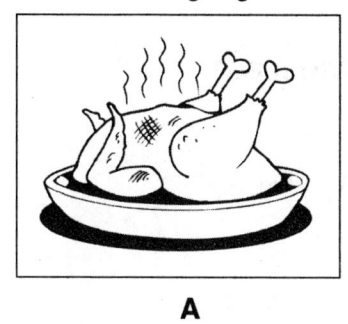

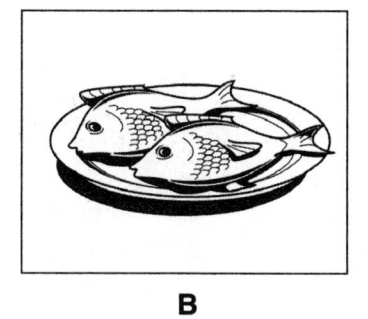

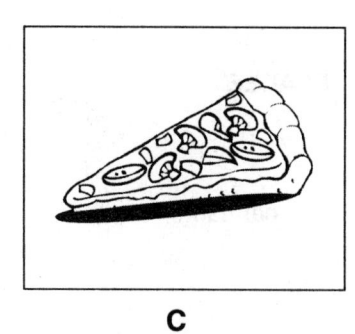

A   B   C

5 What did Jack's mum give him for his birthday?

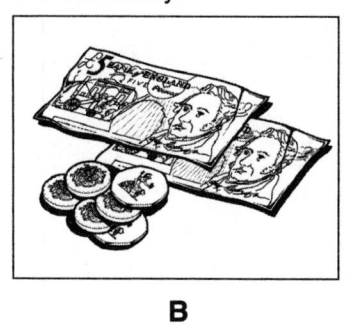

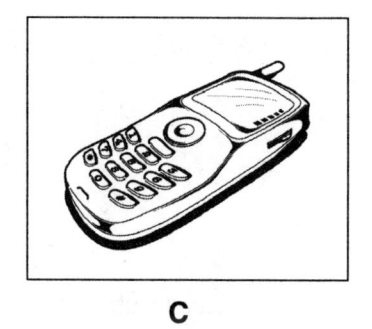

A   B   C

Test 3

PART 2

QUESTIONS 6–10

Listen to Lucy talking to a friend about a new sports centre.
What is the problem with the different places at the sports centre?
For questions **6–10**, write a letter **A–H** next to each place.
You will hear the conversation twice.

Example:

0   swimming pool | C |

PLACES

6   car park   [ ]

7   café   [ ]

8   sports shop   [ ]

9   dance club   [ ]

10 basketball club   [ ]

PROBLEMS

A   big

B   boring

C   crowded

D   dirty

E   early

F   expensive

G   hot

H   small

PART 3

QUESTIONS 11–15

Listen to Simon talking to a friend about a school trip.
For each question, choose the right answer (**A**, **B** or **C**).
You will hear the conversation twice.

Example:

0   Simon went on a school trip on

   A   Monday.

   B   Tuesday.

   (C)   Wednesday.

---

11   In the morning, Simon visited the

   A   science museum.

   B   motorbike factory.

   C   TV centre.

12   Simon thought the TV centre was too

   A   hot.

   B   crowded.

   C   noisy.

13   Simon bought

   A   a T-shirt.

   B   a sandwich.

   C   a poster.

14 Simon enjoyed listening to a talk about

    A music.

    B space travel.

    C clocks.

15 Simon took photographs of

    A a park.

    B his friends.

    C a motorbike.

PART 4

QUESTIONS 16–20

You will hear a girl speaking on the telephone.
Listen and complete each question.
You will hear the conversation twice.

Message

To: Amy

From: (16) ....

About: Shopping trip

Leave at: (17) .... a.m.

Travel by: (18) ....

Take: (19) .... things

(20) and ....

PART 5

QUESTIONS 21–25

You will hear a man talking on the radio about a competition to win concert tickets.
Listen and complete each question.
You will hear the information twice.

Radio Competition to win Concert Tickets

Win tickets to see: Metro

Date of concert: (21) ....

Place: (22) ....

Type of music: (23) ....

Phoning the radio programme

Phone number: (24) ....

Last day to phone: (25) ....

You now have 8 minutes to write your answers on the answer sheet.

PAPER 3 SPEAKING (8–10 minutes)

The Speaking test lasts 8 to 10 minutes. You will take the test with another candidate. There are two examiners, but only one of them will talk to you. The examiner will ask you questions and ask you to talk to the other candidate.

Part 1 (5–6 minutes)

The examiner will ask you and your partner some questions. These questions will be about your daily life, past experience and future plans. For example, you may have to speak about your school, hobbies or home town.

Part 2 (3–4 minutes)

You and your partner will speak to each other. You will ask and answer questions. The examiner will give you a card with some information on it. The examiner will give your partner a card with some words on it. Your partner will use the words on the card to ask you questions about the information you have. Then you will change roles.

Test 4

PAPER 1 READING AND WRITING (1 hour 10 minutes)

PART 1

QUESTIONS 1–5

Which notice (A–H) says this (1–5)?
For questions 1–5, mark the correct letter A–H on your answer sheet.

Example:

0 You cannot talk in here.   *Answer:* [0 A B C D E F ■ H]

---

1 This may be the cheapest place to buy these.

2 You should put everything back in the right place.

3 You cannot buy anything here today.

4 If you have lost a book, go and see this person.

5 You can listen to a writer here.

A Dictionary found
See school secretary

B Ask at reception before putting anything on the noticeboard

C **Study Centre**
Return books / CDs to correct shelf after use

D **City Library – TODAY**
Richard Holt will read from his latest book

E **All Students**
Return textbooks to teachers at end of term

F **Today only**
All children's books half-price

G ALL STUDENTS
Please be quiet in the library

H COLLEGE BOOKSHOP
CLOSED UNTIL MONDAY

PART 2

QUESTIONS 6–10

Read the sentences about Emily's birthday.
Choose the best word (**A**, **B** or **C**) for each space.
For questions **6–10**, mark **A**, **B** or **C** on your answer sheet.

Example:

0   Yesterday, Emily was very .... because it was her fourteenth birthday.

   A happy   **B** afraid   **C** surprised   *Answer:* 0 **A** ■ B □ C □

---

6   Emily's parents gave her a new bicycle which she can .... to school every day.

   A go   **B** drive   **C** ride

7   Emily .... three of her friends to meet her in town.

   A agreed   **B** invited   **C** explained

8   Emily and her friends had a .... in a café and then they went shopping.

   A meal   **B** food   **C** dish

9   Emily and her friends then .... the evening watching a DVD at her house.

   A gave   **B** spent   **C** took

10 Emily said it was the most .... birthday ever.

   A favourite   **B** popular   **C** exciting

PART 3

QUESTIONS 11–15

Complete the five conversations.
For questions **11–15**, mark **A**, **B** or **C** on your answer sheet.

Example:

0

Where do you come from?

A New York.
B School.
C Home.

Answer: 0 ■ A □ B □ C

---

11 Shall I make some hot chocolate?

A Yes, of course it is.
B I do too.
C That's a good idea.

12 I thought the film was really boring.

A If you like.
B So did I.
C I'm afraid not.

13 Are you free this Tuesday?

A Not very often.
B Not until the evening.
C Not long now.

14 I'll wait for you outside the stadium.

A Can we meet somewhere else?
B Do you know how to do it?
C Are you sure you went there?

15 Have you got this T-shirt in a larger size?

A I haven't seen it.
B I think you will be.
C I'll go and check for you.

QUESTIONS 16–20

Complete the conversation between two friends.
What does Luke say to David?
For questions **16–20**, mark the correct letter **A–H** on your answer sheet.

Example:

David: Hi, Luke. Do you want to come and watch the hockey game this evening?

Luke: 0 .....C.....

Answer: 0 [C marked]

David: Good. Let's meet in the entrance to the sports hall.

Luke: **16** ....

David: It doesn't begin until seven, but can you get there by six?

Luke: **17** ....

David: We'll get good seats at the front if we do that.

Luke: **18** ....

David: I don't know yet, but they won't be expensive.

Luke: **19** ....

David: Yes! I spoke to them this afternoon. Do you know anyone else who would like to come?

Luke: **20** ....

David: OK. I'll call him now.

A Great idea! How much are the tickets?

B No, that bus goes at twenty past.

C Yes, that sounds great!

D That's good. Are Pat and Thomas going too?

E I think John really enjoys watching hockey.

F Me too! I'll have time to buy a burger in town.

G OK. When does the game start?

H That's not a problem. But why so early?

PART 4

QUESTIONS 21–27

Read the article about a career in film and then answer the questions.

Are sentences **21–27** 'Right' **(A)** or 'Wrong' **(B)**?

If there is not enough information to answer 'Right' **(A)** or 'Wrong' **(B)**, choose 'Doesn't say' **(C)**.

For questions **21–27**, mark **A**, **B** or **C** on your answer sheet.

Would you like a career in film?

Lana Carter has not worked in film for many years but she has already helped make several movies and worked with a few famous film stars.

Lana's job is to work the lights and the camera during filming. Sometimes, she also helps decide where movies are made. She has worked on all kinds of full-length movies and a variety of advertisements and music videos. She thinks making music videos is the easiest because they don't have to look or feel real. She says that working on movies is more difficult because lighting mistakes can make the whole thing look wrong.

Lana decided she would like to work in film when she was 16. Her friends and family laughed at the idea, but she found out about courses and did a university course in Film and Video. She says, 'You shouldn't worry about making mistakes at university. Try new ideas and don't just do the same as everyone else.' She thinks that people who want a career like hers should choose a course that lets them do as much filming as possible. 'Courses that just ask students to do a lot of writing are not useful to anybody.'

Example:

0   Lana Carter has had a long career in film.

  A Right **B** Wrong **C** Doesn't say   *Answer:* 0 A ■ C

---

21   Lana has met some famous actors.

  A Right **B** Wrong **C** Doesn't say

22   Lana likes planning where to make films most of all.

  A Right **B** Wrong **C** Doesn't say

23   Lana believes that music videos are harder to make than movies.

  A Right **B** Wrong **C** Doesn't say

24   Lana's family wanted her to have a career in film.

  A Right **B** Wrong **C** Doesn't say

25   Lana was one of the best students on her course at university.

  A Right **B** Wrong **C** Doesn't say

26   Lana thinks it is fine for film students to make mistakes.

  A Right **B** Wrong **C** Doesn't say

27   Lana thinks that writing is more important on courses than making films.

  A Right **B** Wrong **C** Doesn't say

PART 5

QUESTIONS 28–35

Read the article about basketball.
Choose the best word (**A**, **B** or **C**) for each space.
For questions **28–35**, mark **A**, **B** or **C** on your answer sheet.

Basketball

Today, Americans watch more basketball **(0)** .... television than any other sport. But it is popular in **(28)** .... countries too. People often **(29)** .... it 'the international game' because it is played in almost **(30)** .... country of the world. But basketball is not an old sport like football, which people have played for centuries. People have only played basketball **(31)** .... 1891.

The idea for basketball came from James Naismith, a Canadian teacher, who wanted his students to learn **(32)** .... new kind of sport. Instead **(33)** .... the players kicking the ball **(34)** .... they do in soccer, in Naismith's new game, the players threw or bounced the ball. Then, they had to get **(35)** .... into a big bag or 'basket'. The name that Naismith chose for this new sport was 'basketball'.

Example:

| 0 | A | on | B | in | C | to | *Answer:* | 0 A■ B☐ C☐ |

| 28 | A | another | B | both | C | other |

| 29 | A | called | B | call | C | calling |

| 30 | A | every | B | both | C | some |

| 31 | A | before | B | since | C | until |

| 32 | A | a | B | the | C | one |

| 33 | A | at | B | from | C | of |

| 34 | A | if | B | as | C | for |

| 35 | A | it | B | him | C | them |

Test 4

PART 6

QUESTIONS 36–40

Read the descriptions of some things you may see in the countryside.
What is the word for each one?
The first letter is already there. There is one space for each other letter in the word.
For questions **36–40**, write the words on your answer sheet.

Example:

| 0 | These fall from trees in the autumn when the weather gets colder. | l _ _ _ _ _ |

Answer: | 0 | leaves |

36 This grows on the ground and horses and sheep eat it.   g _ _ _ _ _

37 You usually see lots of tall trees in this place.   f _ _ _ _ _ _

38 You need to stand on a hill on a windy day to fly this.   k _ _ _

39 People come here to go fishing.   r _ _ _ _

40 This is very high and it can take a long time to walk to the top.   m _ _ _ _ _ _ _

82

PART 7

QUESTIONS 41–50

Complete the email.

Write ONE word for each space.

For questions **41–50**, write the words on your answer sheet.

Example: | 0 | in |

| From: | Patrick |
| To: | Karl |

Hi!

At the moment I'm on holiday **(0)** .... Jamaica with my parents. We flew to this wonderful island two weeks **(41)** .... It is sunny every day. **(42)** .... week we saw most of the island because my dad rented a car.

We **(43)** .... staying at a lovely hotel **(44)** .... a swimming pool, but we often swim in the sea instead. I love swimming there because **(45)** .... water is so clear. I swam quite a long way yesterday and saw a **(46)** .... of beautiful fish. **(47)** .... were some amazing red and yellow fish and I took pictures of them.

Jamaica is **(48)** .... beautiful than anywhere else I've been to, and I don't want **(49)** .... come home! But school starts again at the end **(50)** .... August. So I'll see you then!

Patrick

Test 4

PART 8

QUESTIONS 51–55

Read the advertisement and the email.

Fill in the information in Jo's notes.

For questions **51–55**, write the information on your answer sheet.

Star Phones
11 Market Street

SALE

Starts: 29 July
Finishes: 5 August

Mobile phones £55
– were £120

From:	Mike
To:	Jo

I know you want a new mobile so why don't we go to Star Phones, the store on Market Street, not the one on Bridge Street, on the first day of their sale? Their phones will be £65 cheaper then. There's a bus to the city centre at 8.10 so wait for me at the library at 7.45 and we'll walk to the bus station together.

Jo's Notes

Shopping Trip

Name of shop: Star Phones

Date of trip: **51**

Address of shop: **52**

Sale price of phones: **53** £

Place to meet Mike: **54**

Time bus leaves: **55** a.m.

PART 9

QUESTION 56

Read the email from your English friend, Robin.

From:	Robin
To:	

I really like listening to music. What kind of music do you like? Who is your favourite band? How many of their CDs do you have?

Write an email to Robin and answer the questions.
Write **25–35** words.
Write the email on your answer sheet.

PAPER 2   LISTENING   (approximately 30 minutes including 8 minutes transfer time)

PART 1

QUESTIONS 1–5

You will hear five short conversations.
You will hear each conversation twice.
There is one question for each conversation.
For each question, choose the right answer (**A**, **B** or **C**).

Example:

Which is the girl's horse?

A (circled)   B   C

---

1   What is Becky going to take for the picnic?

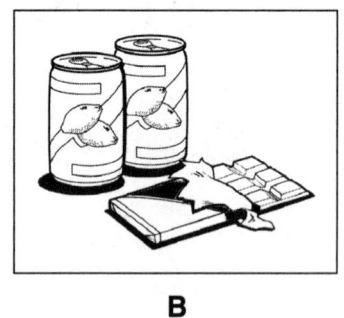

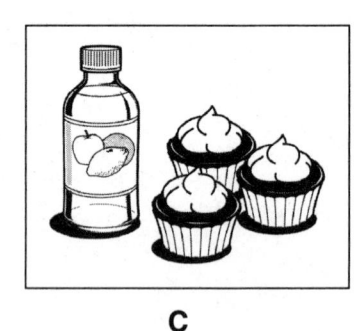

A   B   C

2   How much is the mobile phone?

£30   £55   £75

A   B   C

3 Where will they buy the eggs?

A    B    C

4 What time does the film start?

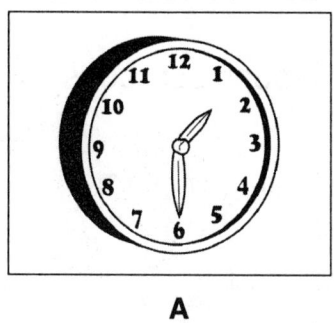

A 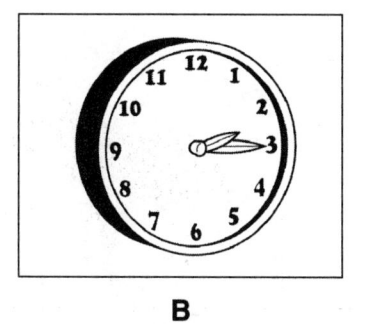   B 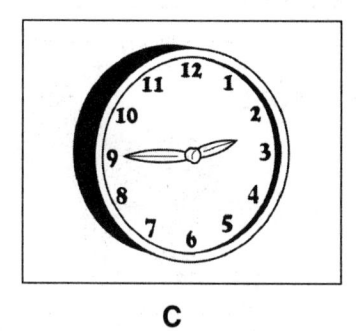   C

5 How will the boy travel to the beach?

A    B 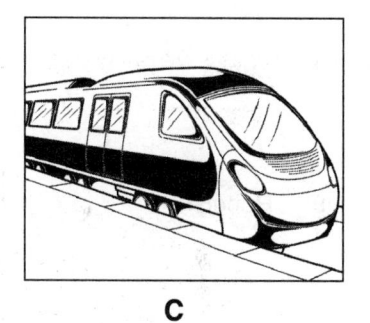   C

Test 4

PART 2

QUESTIONS 6–10

Listen to Rick and Helen talking about their friends and their favourite lessons.
What is each person's favourite lesson?
For questions **6–10**, write a letter **A–H** next to each person.
You will hear the conversation twice.

Example:

0   Helen | G |

PEOPLE

6   Rick   ☐

7   Paul   ☐

8   Sunita   ☐

9   Robert   ☐

10   Holly   ☐

FAVOURITE LESSONS

A   art

B   English

C   geography

D   history

E   maths

F   music

G   science

H   Spanish

Paper 2 Listening

PART 3

QUESTIONS 11–15

Listen to Joe talking to his mother about his day at school.
For each question, choose the right answer (**A**, **B** or **C**).
You will hear the conversation twice.

Example:

0   What time did Joe get home?

    A   3.45 p.m.

   (B)   4.00 p.m.

    C   4.15 p.m.

---

11   Where did Joe play football?

    A   in the park

    B   in the sports hall

    C   on the school field

12   Joe would like his mother to wash his

    A   socks and shorts.

    B   T-shirt and shorts.

    C   socks and T-shirt.

13   When is Joe's next football match?

    A   12 March

    B   15 March

    C   18 March

14 The team photo will cost Joe

    A £2.25.

    B £4.50.

    C £6.75.

15 What homework must Joe do for tomorrow?

    A science

    B history

    C maths

PART 4

QUESTIONS 16–20

You will hear a girl, Lucy, talking to a friend about visiting the cinema.
Listen and complete each question.
You will hear the conversation twice.

Cinema Visit

Name of cinema:	Star Cinema
Day of cinema visit:	(16) ....
Name of film:	(17) ....
Place to meet:	(18) ....
Time film begins:	(19) .... p.m.
Cost of my ticket:	(20) £ ....

PART 5

QUESTIONS 21–25

You will hear a teacher talking about a trip to the zoo.
Listen and complete each question.
You will hear the information twice.

Zoo Trip

Name of zoo:	Westpark Zoo
Day of trip:	(21) ....
Cost of trip:	(22) £ ....
Meeting place for tour:	(23) ....
At 3 p.m. see:	(24) .... eat their food
Zoo shop sells:	(25) .... and postcards

You now have 8 minutes to write your answers on the answer sheet.

PAPER 3 SPEAKING (8–10 minutes)

The Speaking test lasts 8 to 10 minutes. You will take the test with another candidate. There are two examiners, but only one of them will talk to you. The examiner will ask you questions and ask you to talk to the other candidate.

Part 1 (5–6 minutes)

The examiner will ask you and your partner some questions. These questions will be about your daily life, past experience and future plans. For example, you may have to speak about your school, hobbies or home town.

Part 2 (3–4 minutes)

You and your partner will speak to each other. You will ask and answer questions. The examiner will give you a card with some information on it. The examiner will give your partner a card with some words on it. Your partner will use the words on the card to ask you questions about the information you have. Then you will change roles.

Visual materials for Paper 3

1A

Future World
the amazing new computer game
Build a city in space

On Sale
from next week
in
computer shops and supermarkets

For 2–4 players
only £35!

2B

Ride at Adventure Park

- name / ride ?
- when / open ?
- what / see ?
- children's ticket ? £ ?
- where / buy tickets ?

3A

Free Lesson

Do you know how to repair your bike?

Sarah can teach you!

Come to 'The Bike Shop'

140 West Street

10 a.m. Saturday

Bring your bike!

4B

Singing competition

- when ?
- where ?
- age / singers ?
- what / win ?
- more information ? ☎ ?

Visual materials

1B

Computer game

- what / called ?

- expensive ?

- how many players ?

- where / buy ?

- buy / now ?

2A

New ride opens 5 May
at Adventure Park
See all the city from
The Big Wheel

Tickets on sale at park entrance
Adults: £3.50
Under 16s: £2.50

3B

Free lesson

- what / learn ?
- name / teacher ?
- where / lessons ?
- time ?
- take anything ?

4A

COMPETITION
Young Singer of the Year

York Concert Hall

May 29

Win a guitar!

Singers must be under 16

Want to know more? Call or text 998456

TeenVoice

the new magazine for teenagers
£2

interesting stories and pages of fashion and music
on sale every week

go to
www.teenvoice.com
NOW

Jeep ride

- where ?
- for children ?
- every day ?
- price ? £ ?
- what / wear ?

3C

Black's English School

29 Park Street

Learn to speak English in 2 hours a week

Beginners: 6 p.m. – 8 p.m. Wednesdays
Conversation classes: 9 a.m. – 11 a.m. Saturdays

£60 for 6 lessons

Call: 321703

4D

Television music channel

- name / channel ?
- what kind / music ?
- date / start ?
- what / see ?
- website ?

1D

Teenage magazine

- name / magazine ?

- website ?

- what / read about ?

- cost ? £ ?

- when / buy ?

2C

Jeep Rides
in the desert

Tuesdays and Saturdays
2 p.m. till 6 p.m.

£17.50 per person

Children must be over 12 years old

Bring hat and boots

3D

English lessons

- where ?

- conversation classes ?

- cost ?

- how long / lesson ?

- more information ? ☎ ?

4C

A great new TV channel:

MUSIC CHANNEL PLUS

starts 1 May

watch the latest music videos
and
listen to rock and hip-hop

visit **www.music.com** for more information

Sample answer sheet - Reading and Writing (Sheet 1)

UNIVERSITY of CAMBRIDGE
ESOL Examinations

SAMPLE

Candidate Name
If not already printed, write name in CAPITALS and complete the Candidate No. grid (in pencil).

Candidate Signature

Examination Title

Centre

Supervisor:
If the candidate is ABSENT or has WITHDRAWN shade here

Centre No.

Candidate No.

Examination Details

KET Paper 1 Reading and Writing Candidate Answer Sheet

Instructions

Use a PENCIL (B or HB).
Rub out any answer you want to change with an eraser.

For **Parts 1, 2, 3, 4 and 5**:
Mark ONE letter for each question.
For example, if you think **C** is the right answer to the question, mark your answer sheet like this:

| 0 | A B C |

Part 1
1. A B C D E F G H
2. A B C D E F G H
3. A B C D E F G H
4. A B C D E F G H
5. A B C D E F G H

Part 2
6. A B C
7. A B C
8. A B C
9. A B C
10. A B C

Part 3
11. A B C
12. A B C
13. A B C
14. A B C
15. A B C
16. A B C D E F G H
17. A B C D E F G H
18. A B C D E F G H
19. A B C D E F G H
20. A B C D E F G H

Part 4
21. A B C
22. A B C
23. A B C
24. A B C
25. A B C
26. A B C
27. A B C

Part 5
28. A B C
29. A B C
30. A B C
31. A B C
32. A B C
33. A B C
34. A B C
35. A B C

Turn over for Parts 6 - 9 →

© UCLES 2010 Photocopiable

Sample answer sheet - Reading and Writing (Sheet 2)

For **Parts 6, 7 and 8**:
Write your answers in the spaces next to the numbers (36 to 55) like this:

0	example

Part 6	Do not write here
36	1 36 0
37	1 37 0
38	1 38 0
39	1 39 0
40	1 40 0

Part 7	Do not write here
41	1 41 0
42	1 42 0
43	1 43 0
44	1 44 0
45	1 45 0
46	1 46 0
47	1 47 0
48	1 48 0
49	1 49 0
50	1 50 0

Part 8	Do not write here
51	1 51 0
52	1 52 0
53	1 53 0
54	1 54 0
55	1 55 0

Part 9 (Question 56): Write your answer below.

Do not write below (Examiner use only)
0 1 2 3 4 5

Sample answer sheet - Listening

UNIVERSITY of CAMBRIDGE
ESOL Examinations

S A M P L E

Candidate Name
If not already printed, write name in CAPITALS and complete the Candidate No. grid (in pencil).

Candidate Signature

Examination Title

Centre

Supervisor:
If the candidate is ABSENT or has WITHDRAWN shade here

Centre No.

Candidate No.

Examination Details

KET Paper 2 Listening Candidate Answer Sheet

Instructions

Use a **PENCIL** (B or HB).

Rub out any answer you want to change with an eraser.

For **Parts 1, 2** and **3**:
Mark ONE letter for each question.
For example, if you think **C** is the right answer to the question, mark your answer sheet like this:

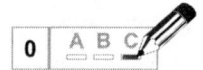

| 0 | A B C |

Part 1
1. A B C
2. A B C
3. A B C
4. A B C
5. A B C

Part 2
6. A B C D E F G H
7. A B C D E F G H
8. A B C D E F G H
9. A B C D E F G H
10. A B C D E F G H

Part 3
11. A B C
12. A B C
13. A B C
14. A B C
15. A B C

For **Parts 4** and **5**:
Write your answers in the spaces next to the numbers (16 to 25) like this:

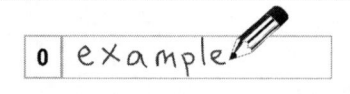

| 0 | example |

Part 4		Do not write here
16		1 16 0
17		1 17 0
18		1 18 0
19		1 19 0
20		1 20 0

Part 5		Do not write here
21		1 21 0
22		1 22 0
23		1 23 0
24		1 24 0
25		1 25 0

© UCLES 2010 Photocopiable